Minivanity

An Adam Collection
by Brian Basset

Andrews and McMeel
A Universal Press Syndicate Company
Kansas City

ISBN: 0-8362-0417-4

Library of Congress Catalog Card Number: 95-77572

Other Books by Brian Basset

Adam
Life in the Fast-Food Lane
Life Begins at 6:40

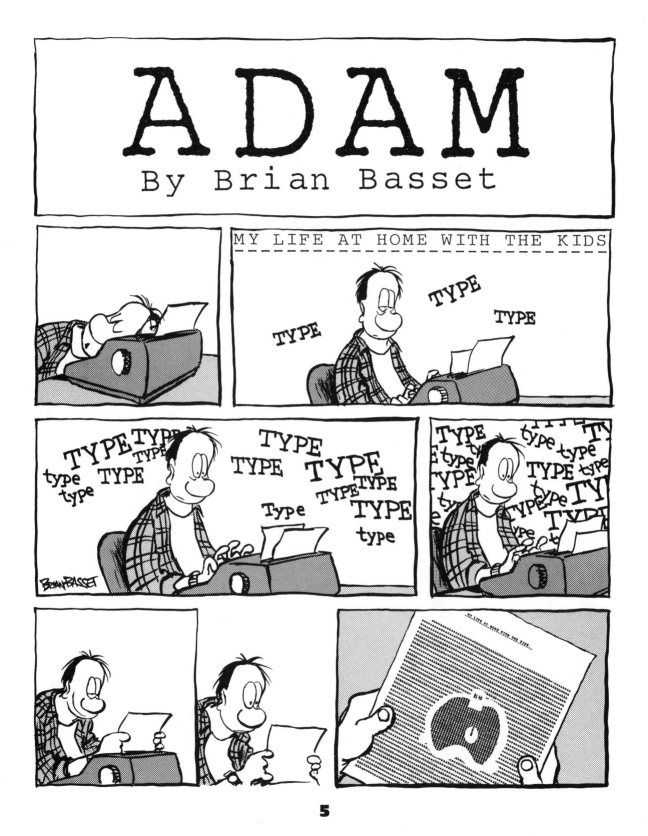

6

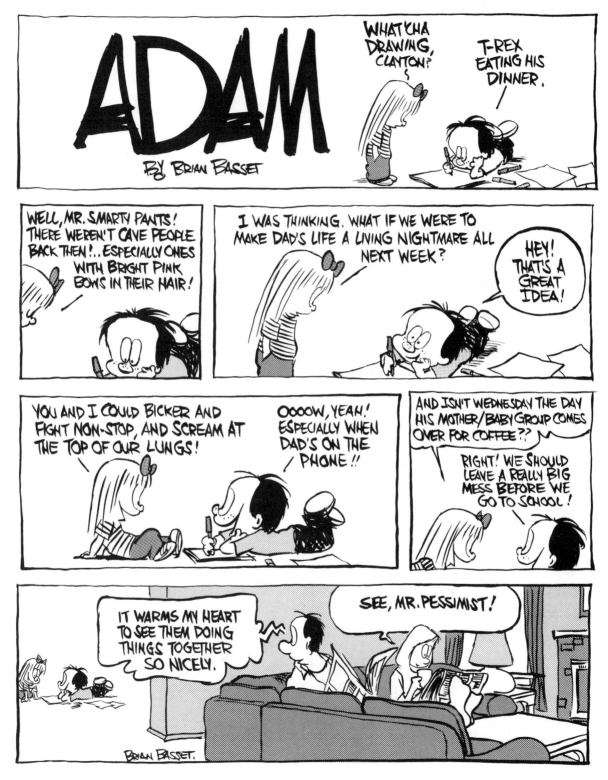

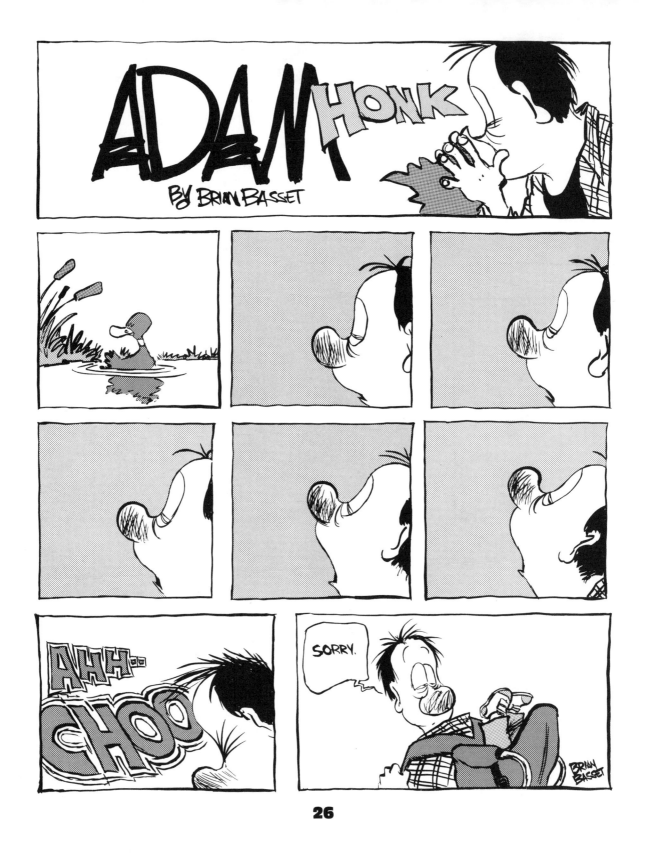

32

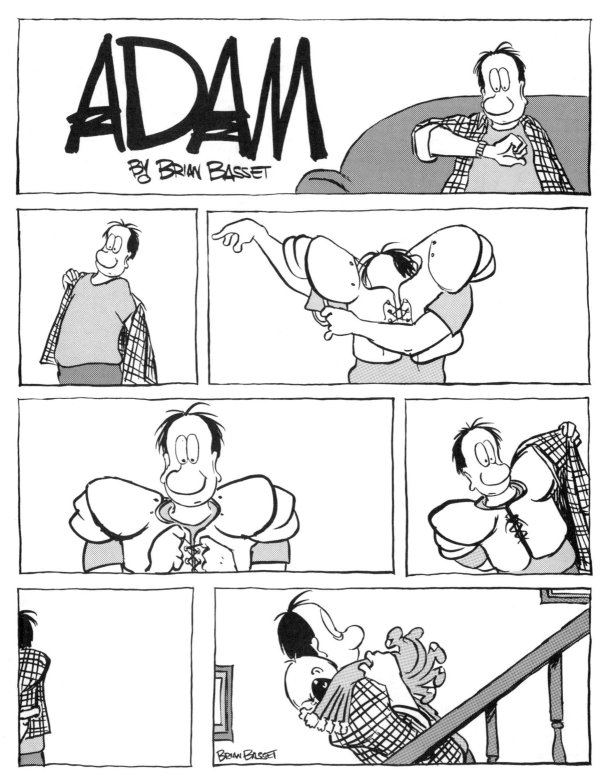

48

51

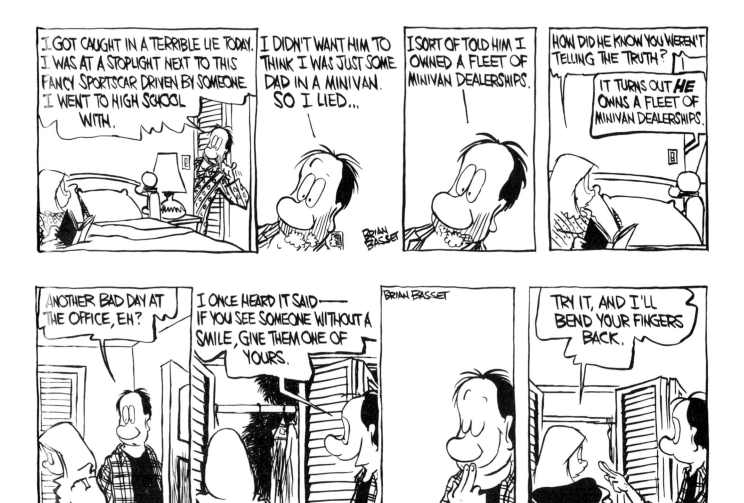

I GOT CAUGHT IN A TERRIBLE LIE TODAY. I WAS AT A STOPLIGHT NEXT TO THIS FANCY SPORTSCAR DRIVEN BY SOMEONE I WENT TO HIGH SCHOOL WITH.

I DIDN'T WANT HIM TO THINK I WAS JUST SOME DAD IN A MINIVAN. SO I LIED...

I SORT OF TOLD HIM I OWNED A FLEET OF MINIVAN DEALERSHIPS.

HOW DID HE KNOW YOU WEREN'T TELLING THE TRUTH?

IT TURNS OUT *HE* OWNS A FLEET OF MINIVAN DEALERSHIPS.

ANOTHER BAD DAY AT THE OFFICE, EH?

I ONCE HEARD IT SAID— IF YOU SEE SOMEONE WITHOUT A SMILE, GIVE THEM ONE OF YOURS.

BRIAN BASSET

TRY IT, AND I'LL BEND YOUR FINGERS BACK.

WELL, IT DIDN'T TAKE LONG. OUR NEW MINIVAN DOESN'T HAVE THAT NEW CAR SMELL ANYMORE.

IT NOW HAS THAT FRENCH FRY GROUND INTO THE SEAT, SPILLED CHOCOLATE SHAKE, AND ORANGE JOLLY RANCHER STUCK TO THE FLOOR AND CEILING SMELL.

ORANGE ISN'T SO BAD.

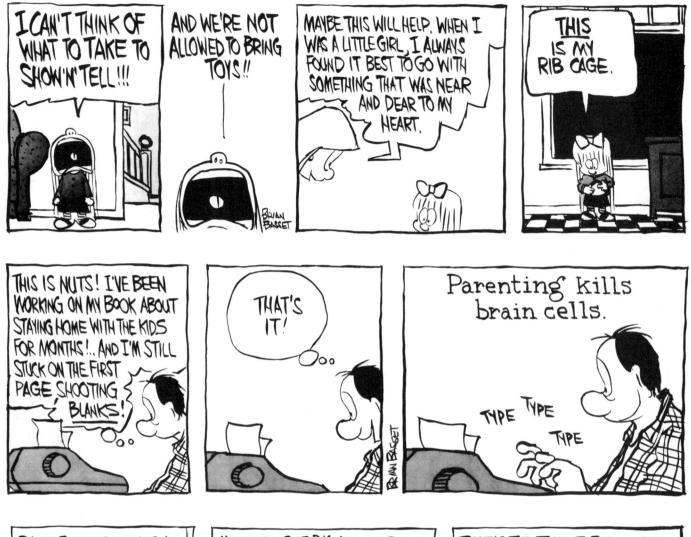

74

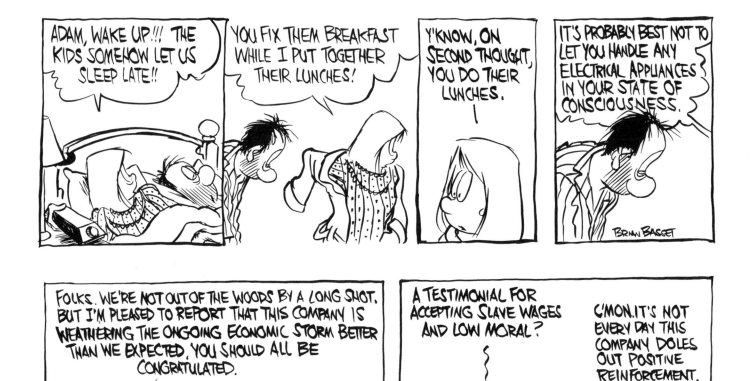

89

IT'S WEIRD. I'M EATING LESS AND EXERCISING MORE, YET I DON'T FEEL, Y'KNOW, ENERGIZED.

I'VE ALWAYS WONDERED ABOUT THAT THEORY. IT SEEMS COUNTERPRODUCTIVE.

IF YOU WERE A CAR, WOULD YOU PUT *LESS* GAS IN THE TANK TO DRIVE *MORE*? OF COURSE NOT.

WELL, I WOULD IF I WERE A CAR!... 'CAUSE I'D BE A SPORTY LITTLE RAGTOP, NOT SOME LUMBERING MINIVAN LIKE I DRIVE *NOW*!!

SORRY I BROUGHT IT UP.

LAURA, SINCE MONEY'S TIGHT THIS MONTH, OK IF I SEE A MOVIE TOMORROW NIGHT?

ASIDE FROM NOT PAYING FOR SITTING, HOW DOES THAT HELP OUR FINANCES?

YOU WON'T NEED TO SEE IT. I'LL TELL YOU ALL ABOUT IT WHEN I GET HOME.

CLAYTON! KATY! GET YOUR SHOES AND COATS ON. WE'RE GOING OUT TO DINNER.

WERE YOU ABLE TO GET RESERVATIONS?

YUP, PLUS I GOT TABLE SIX AND SPACE 18.

SPACE 18??

YEAH. REMEMBER THE LAST TIME WE ATE AT THIS PLACE?..CLAYTON THREATENED TO BARF IF WE EVER TOOK HIM BACK THERE.

SO I RESERVED PARKING SPACE 18. THAT WAY WE'LL STILL HAVE A GOOD VIEW OF HIM WHILE WE EAT AND HE STAYS IN THE CAR.

THAT MEANS I'LL STILL HAVE A VIEW OF THE FOOD!

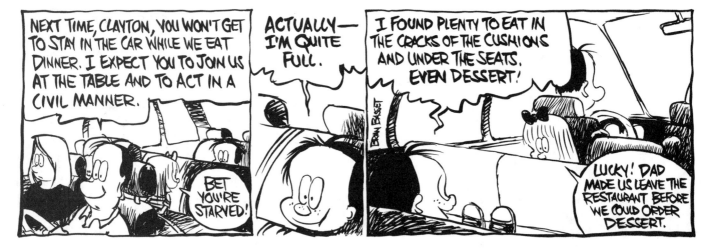

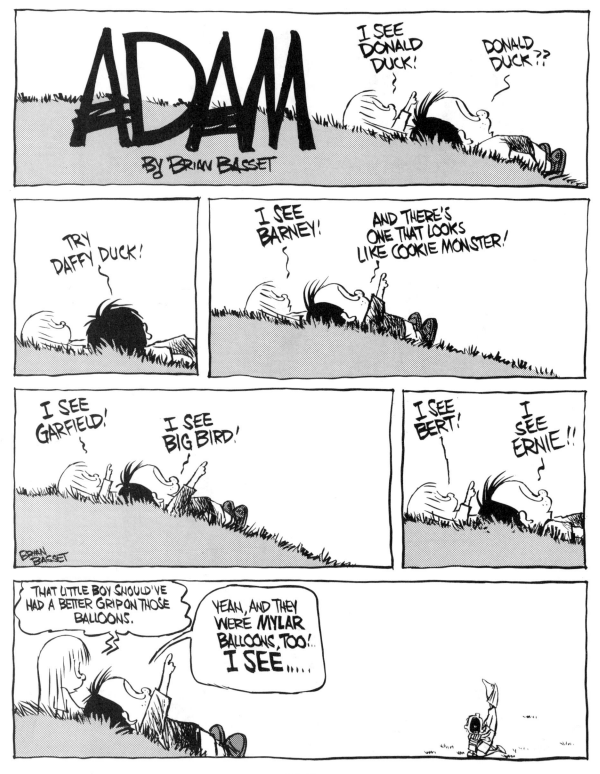

THE END